Main Street-Colorado.com

Business Training Series

CRSO

S0 YOU WANT TO DESIGN, PRINT AND SELL T-SHIRTS!!

CRSO

Professional Instruction By

Timothy M. Braun
&
Anita M. Braun

www.MainStreet-Colorado.com

Sangre de Cristo Publishing, Inc.
Cripple Creek, Colorado

Printed in the United States of America.

Cover design by Timothy M. Braun

Published by Sangre de Cristo Publishing, Inc.,

P.O. Box 1003,

Cripple Creek, CO. 80813

S0 YOU WANT TO DESIGN, PRINT AND SELL T-SHIRTS!!

How To Be in Business in a Short Time for Under $900

You don't have to be a brain surgeon to start a t-shirt business. It's not easy, but it's not hard... it just takes a lot of work and a commitment to be in business for yourself. It's fun, especially when everything comes together and you start getting orders, and some will be large, large enough to pay for all your costs and you can start making a profit.

Do you have a retail business and would like to add custom-made manufactured T-Shirts and Sweatshirts to your line that your customers would love and need? Would you like a GREAT home business manufacturing your own products that are needed and customers love? Why sell someone else's products when you can sell your own? You can wholesale or retail for the greater profit. Advertise your products as ***Made In America!*** Most national brands can't say or do that as most are manufactured overseas. Many customers will pay a premium for anything made in America.

Would you like to be at the top? Would you like to make $$ and REALLY control your own destiny?

Whether you are a stay-at-home mom or dad, retired, handicapped or whatever, you can create a business that makes real $$ -- right from your home!

When you manufacture/make your own T-Shirts and Sweatshirts products you can make upwards of 85%+ profits on your products, or upwards of 600-850% ROI (Return on investment) by starting your own line of T-Shirts and Sweatshirts products.

They are easy to produce and we are going to show you everything, step by step! You can literally have fun; even make it a family business, and possibly turn your products into a multi-million dollar business! There are no quotas or goals to meet. Work and learn at your own pace. There are no sales meetings you have to attend, no sales tiers to work towards. Your rewards are the goals you set and reach for yourself. You are your own boss.

If you never take that first step, nothing ever happens. Every time you resist something new, you hinder yourself from achieving anything. Fear actually stops you from going forward, and we understand that. This is an opportunity, a chance to take an opportunity, to connect with someone who has done it and use our experience to take yourself to the next level. Wherever you are today, just start! Take charge of your future!!

1. Do I need any prior knowledge to get started?

A. No, we teach you everything, from the very basics to the technical.

2. Is there a membership or initiation fee?

A: No, the only costs are the supplies you will need to start to manufacture your products.

All businesses have expenses associated with them. You will need to purchase the e-book on the business that interests you and any supplies in order to manufacture the products.

3. What supplies will I need?

A: We suggest you start manufacturing just a few products, get used to the process and then add products as you feel comfortable, obtain orders or want to add to your line.

4. Where do I learn how to manufacture and obtain training?

A. We have videos planned for the future, so until we have our videos finished, you will be able to simply follow the instructions we give you in this book. We provide all the documentation you need for you to refer to. If you have questions, just email or call us.

5. Do I need a business or a sales tax license?

A. If you intend to grow to a business, you should get a business license and if your state has sales tax, a sales tax license. In addition, many wholesalers will have to have a copy of your licenses to sell to you, or may up the price of the items you need because you aren't a business.

6. Can I get started without a business license or sales tax certificate?

A. Yes, you can order many of your supplies to get started, but wherever you are, you are always better off with a business license. You will need a license to sell or to wholesale.

I started off very small. I just wanted to print a few shirts that I had designed for Smart Ass University, a trademark design I now use for shirts and outerwear. As the shirts gained popularity, I branched out into other areas such as hats, tote bags, tea towels, aprons, etc. I let everyone know I could do shirts for them overnight, and that was the key. Everyone wanted shirts NOW! Screen printers can't do that; no one else around could. You'd be surprised at how many people wait until the last minute to order shirts.

A few years ago, I approached two local stores that agreed to carry some of my shirts. They started out with about 6 different designs. In one summer season, they sold approximately 2500 shirts. They kept adding more designs and even asked me to design and print some shirts they wanted to try. That's where you have a leg up on every screen printer. You can design and print a couple of FULL COLOR shirts for anyone for a couple of dollars, basically the cost of the shirts.

A screen printer will charge well over a hundred dollars for a two or three-color design, just for a couple of shirts. That's because they have a large process to go through. It's costly and labor intensive.

You can sit down at a computer, print out a transfer in a couple minutes, press it in a couple more minutes and you're done, with less than a dollar in costs plus the cost of the shirt. Who do you think a customer will go with to try a new design??

I now print thousands of shirts every year, and I have perfected the process, which I am going to share with you here.

I'm going to take you through a process to begin printing shirts that covers most of the experience I have gained and most of the mistakes I have made. There's no need to make the same mistakes, and believe me, some of them were doozies!!

1. Purchasing a Heat Press

You don't have to have an expensive heat press. There are some great informational videos on Youtube.com on buying a used one over the Internet and on E-bay. What you should look for is the top temperature of a least 400 degrees or more (I'll tell you why later) and a timer that will go at least 8 minutes. Look for one that has a pivoting top. It can be a clamshell type, but the top platen should be able to pivot side-to-side and front to back; not much, but it should pivot. Try not to get a clamshell that is rigid and doesn't allow for different thickness side-to-side or front to back if you can avoid it. I bought a pivoting head press 6 years ago for $350 and I still use it today. I also found a heat press that *IS* rigid on the top, but by loosening the bolts on the bottom platen, it pivots on the bottom, which is also fine.

The one thing you will absolutely need, and this is something I figured out years later, is a digital infrared temperature heat gun. They only cost about $20 on Amazon and will save you a tremendous amount of money and frustration. It tells you the temperature of the Heat Press just by pressing a button and aiming it at the heat platen. For the first few years, at certain times, I had problems with the transfer not peeling right. Sometimes the ink didn't transfer all the way and the shirt was ruined. Even if a small spot didn't transfer, the shirt was ruined as you can't re-press it, and sometimes this happened on several shirts in a row. If your press is too hot or not hot enough, you're going to have problems. Big problems!

I would get upset, mad, and confused, as I knew I was doing everything correctly. I didn't know if it was me, the heat press, the shirt, or the ink that was the problem, and you know it always happened when I was in a hurry or I had a limited number of shirts to work with; and it ALWAYS happened with the most expensive shirts like 2X's and 3X's!

Well, then someone suggested I purchase one of these digital infrared temperature heat guns, and what I found out was astonishing! My heat presses were off as much as fifty degrees from what it said the temperature indicator read. It was way overheating my transfers. When I thought it was at 350 degrees, it was at 400 degrees plus!! And that, my friends, will cause any transfer to go bad. It is so hot it actually melts the transfer film so it won't stick to the shirt. I was clueless as to what was causing my problems, because you can't see it. But since I found this simple remedy, I haven't had one problem and haven't lost one shirt (from heat related damage!)

I don't know if the real expensive presses have this problem, but it will pay dividends to be sure your press is at the right temperature!

2. Inks & Printers

The only place I get my inks for printing shirts, etc. is at www.inkjetcarts.us. The owner's name is Ross Hardie and he is

VERY knowledgeable about almost every printer and what printer to use for this type of printing.

In the past I used the Epson Workforce 1100 (WF1100), but Epson has discontinued that model. The replacement was the WF7010. Now they have discontinued that model. I now have the WF7610, which is the same printer as the WF7010, only I needed a good scanner that scans 11 x 17 and this one does that (it also has a fax that I needed). (I'm sure they will update this printer soon, too.) No matter which printer you purchase, it will be good for many years and does not need to be replaced with newer models.

Ross also has the high-heat inks you need for this type of printing. You can use the Epson inks that come with the printer, but the high-heat inks are the best to use. He has many videos on his website on how to install and use the refillable cartridges and all kinds of informational videos for any type of problems you may encounter. He answers all his emails promptly and is an all-around nice guy. You can even call and talk with him if you're in a bind. He sells world-wide and has the items in-stock.

I wrote and asked him about the difference between the Epson 7010 (which I still have) and the 7510/20 and asked him to place the high-heat inks on the same page as the refillable cartridges so anyone reading this wouldn't have to search for the right inks. He wrote back the same day:

Tim,

The most popular printer you should also recommend will be the Epson workforce 7010 as it is the cheapest model in the series and just a printer without the other features of the scanner and ADF. This model does print only and does not have the bells and whistles of the WF7510 or WF7520.

To comply with your request I have made sure that the WF7010, WF7510 and WF7520 categories also have listed;
1) heat transfer inks
2) HEAT Damper Ciss starterkit
3) HEAT Damper Cart starterkit

ALSO OF SPECIAL NOTE WILL BE THE OTHER WORLDWIDE MODELS AVAILABLE;
EUROPE WF-7015 WF-7515 WF-7525
AUSTRALIA/ASIA WF-7010 (YES SAME MODEL NUMBER AS USA BUT DIFFERENT CHIPS) WE WILL LIST THIS MODEL IN A DIFFERENT CATEGORY "WF-7010 AU" ON OUR WEBSITE. AND OTHER MODELS "WF-7510 AU" AND "WF-7520 AU" SAME AS ABOVE BUT DIFFERENT CHIPS.

WE HAVE ALL WORLDWIDE CHIPS IN STOCK AND I WILL COMPLETE THE CATEGORIES THIS WEEKEND AT THE LATEST.

That is the type of service you should expect from anyone you do business with and you should strive to do the same with your customers.

As of April 2018, Epson is now selling the WF-7620 for $199.00 directly from Epson. Epson is always upgrading their printers with new models, so this one may not always be available. It is wide-format, prints up to 13" wide and 19" long, and will use refillable cartridges. You won't need this much area for all of your printing, but when you need it, it's there. Besides, you can gang images easier with large sheets and save money.

The inks are still, as of this printing, $14 for a 120ml bottle, $26 for 240ml and $50 for a 500ml. If you get all four colors in a 240ml, this will last you for 500-1000 shirts, depending on the size of the printouts. You can get the refillable cartridges and four bottles of 120ml high-heat inks for $79.95 plus freight. I just ordered another set today for a new printer I ordered from Epson. While I'm talking about Epson, I have had printers go bad. Epson has been very good about replacing them. Always purchase the extended warranty if you do a lot of printing. It will pay off in the long run.

I have found that the CISS units are not really practical and are sometimes a real pain. I have used them in all my printers in the past, but now I use refillable cartridges. The CISS units are those that use a tank outside of the printer with a tube to an ink cartridge. I was able to find several companies selling these refillable cartridges on Amazon. Since the names change all the time as to which company is selling them, you will have to do a search for "refillable cartridges for Epson 7110" or whatever your printer is. (SEE THE UPDATE AT THE END OF THIS BOOK FOR SOME GREAT INFO ON REFILLABLE CARTRIDGES!!)

Let's discuss for a moment the type of inks we are using— pigmented inks. There are basically two types of inks, pigmented and dye. Dye inks are used in just about every other printer except the Epsons. Pigmented inks use a different print head than dye inks, so you can't use pigmented inks in just any printer. Pigmented inks are considered the best as they sit on top of the paper instead of going into the paper as the dye inks do. They are more vibrant and are used in professional photos and archive photos. They last a lot longer and don't fade as fast as dye inks. Believe me, you will be disappointed if you use dye inks for your shirts!

Some people will ask you, "Aren't your shirts just iron-on decals?" The answer is a big NO!!! We use professional inks with professional transfer paper that is heat pressed at 350 degrees. No iron can get that hot and the iron-on transfers you can buy at a department store or office supply are JUNK!!!

Whether you use the Epson printers I suggested, or go with another type, always get the wide format that will print 11" x 17". If you don't, you're stuck with small printouts and small transfers. I'll discuss this more in the next section.

3. Paper

I've tried several different papers, don't ask which ones because it's been too long ago, but the one I think is the best and easiest to use, plus it has the most vibrant color is JetPro SofStretch. I used to use Red Grid, but started having problems with it, and I found the JetPro to be much easier to work with.

I get it at www.coastalbusiness.com. I found other places advertising a red grid paper, but some were not the same, so be careful.

There is simply no reason to ever purchase 8.5" x 11" paper. Always buy the 11" x 17". You can gang images (place multiple images) on the 11" x 17" to get more out of your paper. Where you may only get one image out of an 8.5" x 11" sheet with a lot of waste, you may get 3-4 of the same image out of an 11" x 17". The cost, as of this writing, for 11" x 17" JetPro is $49.50 for 50 sheets and $90.00 for 100 sheets. I started out with the 100 sheet packages, but now only buy the 500's. If I get 3 images out of a sheet, the cost is only about 30 cents per shirt. Can you beat that?

That difference is all profit you keep and it really pays when you are doing a hundred or so shirts at a time.

If you are using a small format printer (8.5" x 11" sheet), you can still save money by cutting the 11" x 17" sheets in half.

Let me give you a hint here on using the leftover pieces of JetPro or whatever brand you use. I save all pieces that are 3" or more and use them for small or one-line images. Your printer won't accept a 3" piece of image paper, so on the back of the leftover paper, I attach a 8"x 11"sheet of letter-sized paper by taping it onto the leftover piece. It works great and I don't have nearly as much waste! (See photos)

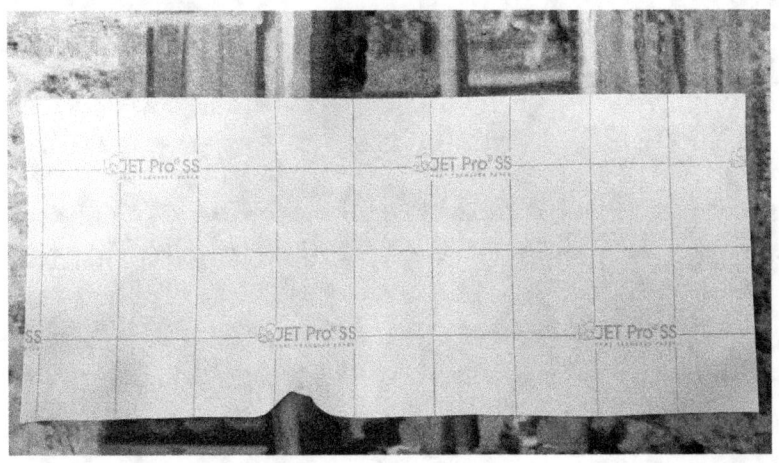

Approximately 4"H x 11"W- Won't go through printer

Approximately 10" x 11" -Will go thru printer

4. Printing

Printing out your transfers should be the easiest part of the process after you have the design down. ALWAYS do a print head check first. It'll save you dollars and time if you have a color that is not printing out 100 percent. Get used to printing only one transfer the first time you print out a design. Inspect it thoroughly before printing more. I've forgotten to reverse the image <u>many</u> times when I get in a hurry, printed out 10-20 of them, walked away to only come back and find they are all trash. Do yourself a favor and follow that rule.

I always use the "Matte" setting on my Epson printers. Matte will give a heavier ink output, which makes your images "POP" more.

Cut out as much as you can around the image without spending a lot of time trying to get it all. Stay about an eighth of inch to a quarter of an inch away from your design or you will eventually cut into it. If you do cut into it, as long as you don't cut a piece out, it's no problem... it won't show up when you press it. As a rule, I don't cut anything out of the interior of an image. The film won't show on most white and natural colored shirts, and will eventually wash out.

Pigment inks take a little longer to dry so be careful when you handle the printouts, as you can smudge them and ruin them. Try not to let them stack up on the printer as they come out if you are using heavy ink coverage, as they can also smudge each other.

5. Pressing Shirts

Now comes the part where you must take the most care. Pre-press each your shirts for at least 5 seconds, longer if you are in a high humidity area. This serves two purposes- it gets rid of any moisture in the shirt that can inhibit a good pressing and eliminates any wrinkles.

One of the largest problems I ever had was I had printed over 100 youth shirts while I was down in Texas on the coast for awhile. I didn't realize the moisture the shirts had picked up from the very high humidity. About a couple weeks after I had shipped them out I got a call saying the transfers were cracking and chipping after washing. I didn't know it was the excess humidity that had caused the problem until later, but if you are in a high humidity area, pre-press the shirts for longer than 5 seconds or until you know the moisture is gone.

At this point, use a lint roller to remove any lint particles that could show up under/in your transfer. You don't want to have a perfect shirt with a red/black piece of lint or string staring at you in the middle of your shirt. (Done that, too)

Do yourself a big favor and purchase a Teflon sheet and a Teflon pillow. It took me quite awhile and a lot of screwed-up shirts to learn that I needed the pillow. These can also be purchased at www.coastalbusiness.com for a reasonable cost. Right now an 18" x 20" sheet goes for about $17.50 and a 16" x 20" pillow for $32.95. Look around and you might be able to find them for less. Coastal also has free freight if you buy $150.00 in merchandise. So if you buy your paper there, get the Teflons also.

(Just to clarify, I have no interest in anyone or anyplace I tell you I purchase at. I receive no kickbacks or special pricing. I am simply telling you where I obtain my supplies.)

Why use the Teflon sheets? If you've ever used the plastisol transfers, you will notice they are on a heavier paper than what you will be using with the ink transfer paper. The ink transfer paper will start to curl the moment it is placed on a hot surface, and your shirt should be hot after you pre-press. This is where the Teflon sheet comes in handy. Placed on top of the paper, it will keep the transfer in place, keep it from moving and keep it from curling. I've lost several shirts because I forgot to put the Teflon on top and the corners or parts of the transfer doubled over on me, creating a mess. When this happens, the shirt is trash and the ink from the fold-over will transfer to the upper heat platen and believe me, it's hard to get it off and clean it.

The sheet is also needed if you have to do two transfers on a shirt at different times, and believe me this will happen. I have shirts that I have already placed a transfer on that I keep in stock. Sometimes a customer will want an additional saying or a city/state also placed on it. **_Never_** press over an image that is on a shirt without placing the Teflon sheet over it. It will stick to the upper heat platen and you will again have another HUGE mess to fix.

Now, what about pressing images on BOTH sides of the shirt? That is where an extra Teflon sheet or the pillow comes in handy. You can immediately turn a shirt over and press another image on the opposite side of a shirt if you use a Teflon sheet/pillow under, too. You don't want your image getting stuck to the rubber on the bottom platen.

The pillow is also needed when you are doing a transfer that will be near the collar or near a seam. On a hard, flat surface or a hard rubber surface, the transfer will not get pressed onto the shirt as hard as it should around those areas and may leave a gap that ruins the shirt. This especially occurs on the back of a shirt if you are pressing high enough that it goes over or near the seam from the front of the shirt. You can also use the pillow inside a shirt or sweatshirt to help press a perfect image over a zippered or buttoned area. Do yourself a BIG favor, avoid a lot of headaches and get one to start out.

**Always** use the heaviest pressure on your heat press you can when pressing your shirts. This will insure the transfer gets pressed into the material as much as possible. A light setting will transfer, but it may crack or peel easily after a wash or two.

Now comes the part where you have to peel the transfer. I found that waiting 2-3 seconds after I take it off the press is best. You can peel the real small items right away off the press, but for the larger ones it pays to wait a few seconds. If you are pressing heavy cotton bags or something like it, I have found that a cold peel is best. You don't have to wait until it is actually cold, but wait a couple minutes. This is for items where the feel of the transfer is not important, as it will have a "heavy" feel.

I have been asked several times about transfers cracking after washing. If you use Red Grid, I spoke to some of the Red Grid people and they told me to stretch the shirt after peeling while it was still hot. I have found a better way. Instead of "Peeling" the transfer off, I grab the shirt or item on both sides and stretch the shirt quickly; I don't really "stretch" the shirt, but more of a "Pop." The paper almost "Pops off" and serves to stretch the transfer also. They are also now suggesting you re-press the transfer (with the Teflon over it) for several seconds after removing the paper.

One other thing you might consider is always attaching a "Care Instructions" label to each shirt you produce. This can reduce problems with washing and ironing. Here is the one I use:

> **Washing and Care Instructions**
> **For best results, always wash in cold water, turn garment inside-out. Do not use chlorine bleach, fabric softener or harsh detergents. Dry on normal heat settings. Do not over dry. Do not iron directly over images.**

This is simply a peal and stick label I put on the outside of the t-shirts or sweatshirts.

6. What and Where to buy shirts

First of all, let's discuss what shirts to use. The inks we use are transparent; that is- they can only be used on light colored shirts. I only offer six colors- white, natural (light brown), light pink, light blue and ash (light grey) in adult shirts and white, light pink and light blue in children's shirts. (I'll talk about children's shirts later). This lets you keep your inventory to a minimum. Believe me, keeping a large number of colors in all the different sizes takes a lot of room, so keep the colors you offer to a minimum to start off with.

Yes, you can offer dark shirts, but it uses an entirely different transfer sheet. They are more expensive and harder to use. It basically places a white background on the shirt so the image you are printing shows up. You won't want to use this unless you are extremely good at cutting around images perfectly or you can use a white square or circle under your image. Give it a try sometime, though, you will see exactly what I'm talking about!

I purchase my shirts from Alphabroder (www.alphabroder.com). If I order by 5 PM, I get the shirts the next day by noon by UPS. Not Bad. Plus, if I order at least $150.00 of non-sale shirts, or $200.00 of sale shirts, the freight is free. This can be a major consideration, as freight can eat your profits up big time. Right now (April 2018), the Gildan G200 (6oz cotton-heaviest cotton) white and natural (light brown) shirts from small to extra large are $1.86 ea in the 6oz cotton, which is the heaviest shirt. The 2X and up are more, at $3.79-$5.84 and up each. You can get 50 shirts to practice on for $93.00, and if you sell a few of them, you can probably pay for all the shirts!

If you were to wholesale 100 shirts for $7 each, that's $700.00 and your cost will be the $186.00 for the shirts, plus 33-50 sheets of transfer 11 x 17 paper plus a couple dollars for ink. That's it! The rest is profit in your pocket, and if you retail them for $12-14 each, you will pocket almost a thousand dollars or more in profit!

Using this type of system, you don't have to keep a huge inventory in, but you should keep a supply level so you can supply anyone that needs a few shirts in a hurry. That's your edge… shirts overnight! At my store, I advertise I can make any shirt in 15 minutes!

7. Marketing

The person was right when he said the best ideas and shirts aren't worth a plug nickel if no one knows about them. Be your own best media and tell everyone you know what you do. You'll be surprised at the response you get. And that doesn't cost a dime. You should have business cards—just be sure to pass them out! Don't be afraid to go to fire and police departments—they give away a lot of shirts to kids. Go to your local bars and nightclubs. I've sold hundreds of shirts to just one bar owner who keeps reordering all the time. All clubs, schools and other organizations use tons of t-shirts and they order all the time. Also consider family reunions, bachelorette/bachelor parties, team walks/runs, small groups that want cohesive looks at an event, etc. Once you have them, and you treat them right, they'll keep coming back to you. If you want to try to get into some retail stores, remember retailers will want at least 50% of the sale of any shirts. So do your homework and see what specialized shirts are going for in your area. They usually range from $12-22.00 depending on the region you are in. In my city, they go for about $14.95, so I wholesale them to retailers at $7.49. Every week, I re-supplied around 50-70 shirts to the two stores I told you about, so I was making several hundred dollars a week just on those.

One big secret here: I was very anxious to get into some **t-shirt stores** in my area, and I when I finally did, my shirts didn't sell as well. Why? Because there were 800 other types of shirts and mine got lost in the mounds of other t-shirts vying for attention. Plus, unless you have shirts that will fly off the shelf, you aren't going to get any primo space.   Try gift stores! That's where I sold 2,500 of them in two stores in one summer in a small town that caters to tourists. Gift stores are always looking for new items and new ideas!

Sublimation

The reason I told you to get a heat press with a pivoting head and 400 degree temperature is this: After you get proficient with t-shirts, you may want to try your hand at sublimation. This goes hand in hand with the marketing of t-shirts and is very profitable in itself. Just about any business you can sell t-shirts to, you can also sell coffee mugs, signs, clocks, etc., to. About the only extra investment you have to make is a mug press, another printer and the special inks and paper needed for that printer for sublimation. (See our e-book on sublimation!)

Design

You don't have to be an expert at computer design. There are many cheap t-shirt design programs you can pick up at office supply stores or online. You can also grab a few software products that have images you can use in your designs. I don't use them as if you read the fine print it usually says they can't be used for commercial purposes.

I have used www.fiverr.com many times to get a design done that I didn't know how to do. It is usually only $5 and some of the designers on there are really good. If you find one that really knows their stuff, stick with him/her and throw a little extra to them once in awhile and they will do wonders for you. I had a logo that was just two colors and basically just a line art. I asked one designer to color it and make it more three-dimensional. He did a

great job and I gave him an extra $10. He was happy and I got
something I would have had to pay hundreds for if I hired someone
at a design company.

CHARTER MEMBER

The left one is what I gave him to work with (2-color); the right one
is what I got for just $5 (Full Color)!! It was a great deal!

I had the following logo done for a cookie store. I told them what I
wanted and she came up with the following. She charged me $20.
I thought it was a real bargain.

Always make sure you have the rights to any photo or logo or design you intend to use. There are many copyrighted label designs out there for sale, so make sure you get the rights to use any design forever.

Always make sure you have the rights to any photo or logo or design you intend to use or print. Always ask your customer if they have the rights to any photo or logos they want to use in a design. There are many copyrighted designs out there for sale, so make sure you get the rights to use any design forever.

Children's Shirts

One last bit of information that is important if you are selling infant or children's shirts. A law was passed called the Consumer Product Safety Improvement Act of 2008, http://www.cpsc.gov/about/cpsia/cpsia.html ,that requires all kinds of testing on children's (up to age 12) wear. Read about the law. I can't give you everything here, but there are big fines for not following it. You can get a waiver from the federal government if you sell less than 1 million dollars a year and I think all of us qualify for that, but all the shirts have to have special labeling. Here is a copy of my waiver from the Feds:

Sangre de Cristo Publishing, Inc.,

The U.S. Consumer Product Safety Commission (CPSC) has accepted your company's registration for the Small Batch Manufacturer Registry.

Small Batch Manufacturer Registration Number: 019794-xxxxxx

This number should be used in your certificate of compliance to identify those products that are considered covered products. Click here for more information.

If you have questions, please e-mail: www.clearinghouse@cpsc.gov, or call (301) 504-7921.

Thank you,

U.S. Consumer Product Safety Commission

So now that you are ready to start your own t-shirt business, let's look at the total cost of a start-up from my experiences I have outlined. This is with the understanding that you already have a computer and a program for designing your shirts.

Epson 7620 printer	$199.99
Refillable cartridges and inks	$74.95
Heat Press	$350.00 (est)
Transfer Paper (100 sheets)	$90.00
Shirts(50 Small-Xlrg)	$93.00
Teflon sheet and Pillow	$50.45
Digital Infrared Thermometer (approx)	$20.00
Total estimate cost of start-up (approx)	**$878.40**

Now, for those of you who've made it this far, I am going to let you in on a little secret; no…, a BIG secret. After I have printed a certain design for a while and know it's selling well and going to sell well in the future, I have the transfers screen printed. Not the shirts, just transfers.

They are printed with plastisol, the same formula as they print on shirts, but they are printed on a release paper. They only take 7 seconds to transfer and at a lower heat.

Go to: www.fmexpressions.com. They will print your one-color transfers for .15 cents each with a $25.00 set-up fee in any color. So, if you have designs or sayings that only use one color, are within a 9" x 12", you can have them made for .15 ea. You can't beat that! You can have a 100 plastisol transfers for $40.00!

They also do full color transfers, up to 9" x 12" for $1.15 each with a $60.00 set-up fee which is waived if you order 300.

This can be a huge savings. I use them a lot as it saves me time on printing out images when I get busy and I have five different people wanting three shirts each.

Where can you start a real business on a budget like that where you have the great possibility of making literally thousands of dollars a year, part-time?

Take care and good luck on your venture. Let your imagination soar as to what you can do and sell. I hope you make lots of money!!

God bless,

Tim Braun

Sangre de Cristo Publishing, Inc.

You can contact me at MainStreetColorado @gmail.com.

UPDATE!!

Ross (at inkjetcart.us) carries the refillable cartridges for the new Epson printers. (WF-7010 series)

I just ordered some of these cartridges from him and found them to be perfect for my Epson printers. Besides that, I found out the cartridges have small batteries in them. I looked at all my old cartridges that didn't work anymore, and, sure enough, all of them had batteries in them. Plus, I found out from Ross that when the cartridges won't reset, it's because the battery is dead, and that the batteries are only supposed to last about 12-18 months! Many of the batteries in the cartridges won't last even 12 months as they have been sitting on a shelf or in storage for months.

Here's the great part…, you can change the batteries, even on most of the cartridges purchased elsewhere. Ross has the new batteries in stock for about 50 cents apiece. He also has a video on how to change the batteries. I watched the video and it only took about two minutes to change the battery and was very easy. You can watch the video here: http://www.inkjetcarts.us/support/article/self-resettable-china-battery-powered-chips-battery-replacement-video-tutorial-112.html

ANOTHER UPDATE...!!!!

The newer Epson printers have new cartridge types! They don't have or need batteries in them! You just take the cartridge out and then place it back in and it's reset!! How great is that! These are the WF-7610 series. I'm hoping any newer models also have the same!

Here are some of my designs that sell really well!

Smart Ass University

GREAT SEAL OF SMART ASS UNIVERSITY

CERTIFIED INSTRUCTOR

I HAVE A.D.D.
But that doesn't
mean I can't.....
OH, LOOK!!
A SQUIRREL!

A Good Marriage
Is Psychological...
One Is Psycho One is Logical
(I'm the Logical One)

I'm So Cute...
I Wonder Who My
REAL Parents are!

IF YOU'RE GOING TO RIDE
MY ASS, PULL MY HAIR
AND YELL MY NAME!

I Can't Believe
My Luck!
I Found a Girl
Who Likes to F...
(Fish!)

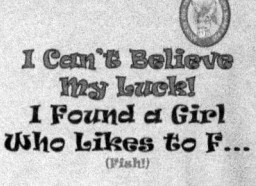

I Have Daughters
I Also Have:
A Gun
A Shovel
A Damn Good Alibi

These are just a few of my shirts hanging in a store.

I just finished printing over 220 shirts for our city's clean-up day for the school kids:

Be sure to visit www.MainStreet-Colorado.com for updates to your book!

Protective Foam "Pillow" with Teflon cover for heat transfers. At: https://www.coastalbusiness.com/protective-foam-pillow-with-teflon-covers-for-heat-transfer-printing-pillow-g.html

Protective Cover Sheet for Heat Press Machines - 18" x 20" -- $17.50 at: https://www.coastalbusiness.com/protective-cover-sheet-for-heat-press-machines-18-x-20-teflon-18-s.html

Etekcity 1022 Digital Laser Infrared Thermometer Temperature Gun--- $19.99 on Amazon

Epson WORKFORCE WF-7610 #252XL Refillable Resettable Ink Cartridges $19.95 a set at: https://store.inkjetcarts.us/wf7610-usa-c1560.aspx

InkJetCarts Epson Durabrite Ultra Compatible Pigment Refill Inks +Heat Transfer Yellow $55.00 a set at:

https://store.inkjetcarts.us/inkjetcarts-epson-durabrite-ultra-compatible-pigment-refill-inks-heat-transfer-yellow-p6314.aspx

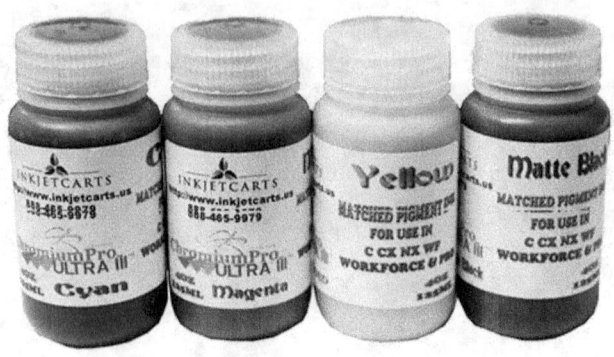